It's In Your Storm

KELSAY DEAN

JOHNSONTRAX PRODUCTIONS & PUBLISHING LLC
Houston, MS

Copyright 2024 by Kelsay Dean

All rights reserved. No portion of this book may be reproduced, stored in a retrieval system, or transmitted in any form or by any means: electronic, mechanical, photocopy, recording, scanning, or other—except for brief quotations in critical reviews or articles, without the written permission of the publisher.

To request permission, contact the publisher at Johnsonsprogress@gmail.com

First Printing: 2024

Paperback: ISBN 979-8-9910318-0-6

JohnsonTrax Productions & Publishing, LLC
Houston, MS 38851
www.unfinishedclay.org

Note: All scripture references are taken from the Holy Bible KJV/NIV Versions

Dedication

This book is in remembrance of my late husband, James Darrell Dean, who passed away last year on April 1, 2023, at the age of 56. He was tragically killed in a tornado that hit our home in the early hours of the morning. James was a loving and devoted husband and father.

Thank You to My Village

To Kaleeyia Stephens, Chrishton Brown, Cheridy Brown, Shaniya Brown, and Leonard Brown, you have all stepped in and done things so selflessly. You have sacrificed your free time; Kaleeyia, you sacrificed your career goals, just for my sake. You have all stepped in without even expecting a thank you. Thank you for remembering all my medications and making sure I get just the right dosages at just the right time of day. I love you all so much, and I could never repay you for the times you have stepped up.

To my best friend, Ambreca Vance, I could never find the words to tell you how much you mean to me. I am eternally grateful for the gift of your friendship in my life. Your unwavering support and understanding have been a true source of comfort and strength. You've been there for me through thick and thin, and I will always cherish your friendship. I am so grateful for your kindness and loyalty.

To my siblings, Tewkunzi Thornton, Ishmuel Stephens, Laketia Petty, and Mattisha Gardner, thank you for always being there for me through the highs and lows. Your presence in my life has been a constant source of comfort. You are my pillar of strength! Thank you for helping me navigate through life's challenges. I am forever grateful.

To my pastors, Bishop Elect Stan Johnson and Evangelist Shalandor Johnson, and my entire church family, House of Mercy was the first place that gave James a sense of "home" after he moved here from Indiana. It's the church where our faith has grown during our 9 years of membership, and it's where we raised our children. Each week during services, I look around and see people I love; people I'm proud to know as my church family. I love you all forever!

I would like to thank all the staff at Shepherd Center, Atlanta, Georgia. A special thank you to my team: Kelsey Lee (OT), Chris Ready (PT),

Deb Eldred (SLP), Cheryl Linden (rehab counselor), Avery Blankenburg (Recreational Therapist), Dr. Wesley Chay, Amanda Morrison (Physician Assistant), Shannon Grizzle (Case Manager), Shannon May (Nurse), Shannon Yates (PCT), Tanis Flagg (PCT), and Martha Murray (Nurse).

To the North Mississippi Medical Center staff (Pontotoc and Tupelo), special thanks to Micki White, who transported me to my husband's funeral. I will always remember you guys!

To Pastor Wright and the cleanup crew, Pontotoc and all surrounding areas, Katina Davis WEAR IT WELL, Chad Mills, the Stephens/Woodard Family, Brownlee/Thompson Family, and my two special friends, Clarisa Brown and Tiffany Harries. Thank you for always being there for me and for being a constant source of support and encouragement. Your friendship means the world to me, and I'm grateful for everything you do.

To my niece KeKe, and to Ascend Therapy, I appreciate you!

To Home Depot, Hero Logistics staff, Toyota Manufacturing, Pontotoc Homes, and the College Hill Community, I appreciate you! Special thanks to Jack & Tiera Crawford and Mechelle Beckley.

Thank you ALL for being my village and comfort!

Table of Contents

Introduction vii

It's In Your Storm 1

    Chapter One 3
    The Storm Will Humble You
    Chapter Two 11
    It Was All a Setup
    Chapter Three 17
    When The Lights Are Out
    Chapter Four 25
    Do It Wounded
    Chapter Five 35
    People Are Watching How You Respond
    Chapter Six 41
    The Promise Doesn't Look So Promising!
    Chapter Seven 47
    Don't Just Be Busy, Be Effective!
    Chapter Eight 51
    Silence The Voices in Your Head
    Chapter Nine 53
    Never Give Up on Your Miracle
    Chapter ten 57
    God Has You Covered
    Conclusion 59
    Life Doesn't Stop for You to Hurt
    About the Author 61

INTRODUCTION

As sure as the sun is going to shine, there are going to be trials and tribulations in our lives. Some may be large and some may be small, yet challenges are sure to come. Going through storms has helped me see more truths about myself than anything has. My storms have given me more power to carry heavier weights and run on longer than I ever have. At some point in life, relationships, finances, health, and morality will be put to the test, and it is in those moments where our character is built.

My trials have shown me who I truly am, and they have given me clarity as to what I possess and what I lack. Waiting for the winds and rain to cease does not feel good, but I have learned that I must not rush it or be so eager to get out of it until I have learned what lesson I need to be taught. It's so sad to say, but I have learned a lot about people too. I have learned that connections are so important when you are going through. It hurts so bad going through this and learning to cut people off in the process, but from me to you, you can't fold. You must stand even when the storm blows harder. You must continue to endure because at the end of the storm, there is a lesson. It wasn't sent to knock you down, but it is trying to teach you to be strong and hold on to your faith and trust God.

Romans 5:4-5 And endurance builds character, which gives us a hope that will never disappoint us. All of this happens because God has given us the Holy Spirit, who fills our hearts with his love.

It's been hard to live this last year, and when I say hard, I mean HARD. A hard that I can't even begin to explain. It cuts deep! Being temporarily paralyzed in a wheelchair, nothing could describe the horror I felt when the doctor said, "You will never walk again." I spent many sleepless nights in the hospital praying, "Oh God, may it not be so!" It's like I heard Him but didn't hear Him if you know what I mean. I never accepted those words He spoke on that day. From the moment He said it, I was still believing the report of the Lord, "By His stripes I am healed." There were some hard days in ICU, but visitors brightened the otherwise miserable days. I was hurt because I had just found out JD had passed. It took my family a few days to let me know that he didn't make it. Each person that came to visit, I would laugh and talk as if nothing was wrong and if nothing had just happened. I was so hurt on the inside, but I felt somewhat a kind of peacefulness like I just knew that God was going to take care of us. My kids were also hurt and suffering from minor cuts and injuries and were living with my sister Tewkunzi, but they came faithfully to visit. My family, friends, church family, and strangers showed up unbelievably for us. The way everyone showed up was just breathtaking.

While in the hospital, my Pastor and First Lady had entered my room. They came directly to my bed where I lay temporarily paralyzed. I remember them walking over to my bed so calmly. They talked freely about God and how He is still a healer! Standing over my bed, my Pastor said, "Kelsay, today is the day you're going to begin your healing." I was stunned by his confident tone of voice. He prayed, and we believed together that x...It's In Your Storm

God was going to heal me. No wheelchair for me! However, I'm still here, and nothing has happened yet. When a month passed, I thought that maybe my healing will happen gradually, but my feet and legs refused to respond to the commands that my mind was proclaiming, "Move, in Jesus's name, move!" When I was released from the hospital in Tupelo, MS (North MS Medical Center), nothing happened. The way I saw it, God was either playing a cruel joke on me, or my view of Scripture was wrong. However, during the time I spent at Shepherd Center in Atlanta, Georgia (one of the greatest Spinal Cord Centers in the country), I came to the realization that the focus of my faith should always be on Jesus and not what He can do for me! I still believe my outer healing will take place, but I now realize that my Pastor was speaking of my inner healing. I should desire His Presence more than what He promised me.

It has been through the darkest seasons of my life that God has done His greatest work. It has been in the dark that I have gained my greatest strengths. For you all, I know being in the storms of life can be intimidating, but God does not use your storms to destroy you. He uses them to develop and elevate you. These are the times that He is developing you if you allow Him to. I've also learned that before I could construct something new, God had to disrupt my old. I had become so complacent and so comfortable, and the disruptions were necessary because He has given me a vision behind them. He disrupted things in my life so that what needed to be constructed could manifest.

A lot of times we don't like to talk about struggling or going through storms, but it's in those times that we are pulled backwards and are able to go forward. God allows things to happen to us on purpose. He won't move until He knows it's too much for us. God will allow us to go to the end of ourselves. When we reach the end of ourselves and our resources, God has a clear path to step in and help. He sometimes allows us to struggle with our problems until we're at our breaking point. He watches as we fight, wrestle, and eventually conclude that we can't handle the situation on our own. That's the moment

He steps in to show His power and reveal His plan. Some people reach this point quickly, while others take longer to surrender. Those who seem stronger often suffer for longer before they finally give up.

It's In Your Storm

2..It's In Your Storm

Chapter One
The Storm Will Humble You

> ❝
>
> ***But he that is greatest among you shall be your servant. And whosoever shall exalt himself shall be abased; and he that shall humble himself shall be exalted.***
> ***Matthew 23:11-12***

Storms can either harden your heart or humble you. They force you to confront your weaknesses and blind spots. God uses them to shape you and prepare you for His purpose. It might not feel good at the time, but it's all part of your growth story. Imagine a life without challenges - you'd be ill-equipped to handle anything difficult. You'd crumble at the first sign of trouble.

Growing up with drug-addicted parents is a tough way to learn about life. I experienced this firsthand. My siblings and I had to fend for ourselves a lot, and I often felt neglected and overlooked.

4..It's In Your Storm

Looking back, it's like those memories are etched in my bones. Growing up with parents who were always getting arrested and always getting high was just... a mess. I remember the drug dealer hiding once in our attic trying to avoid the cops, but he fell right through the roof when the police were almost done searching our house. Man, that was really embarrassing! My mom and dad were in and out of jail, and sometimes we'd stay with Grandma for a little while. However, that didn't really help. We were always wondering where our next meal was coming from or if the water and lights were about to get shut off. It was constant anxiety.

There were times when we fought with our parents because the addictions were too much to bear. This was one of the hardest things we faced. Addiction takes a devastating toll on both the addicts and those who love them. It brings manipulation, guilt, and a constant fear that the person you care about will be lost to their disease.

When someone you love is struggling with addiction, their need for you can feel insatiable. You might find yourself giving money you can't afford, saying yes to dangerous requests, lying to protect them, and feeling your body go cold with fear every time the phone rings in the middle of the night. You want to be there for them, but the thought of seeing them fills you with dread.

It's possible to love an addict and still feel a deep sense of disappointment and frustration. You might stop liking them, but the bond of family or friendship often means you can't completely cut them out of your life. If you're hoping the addict will stop the guilt trips, the lies, and the manipulation, you'll likely be disappointed. Addicts can't make the healthy choices they need to in order to better themselves. The hardest realization comes when you must admit there's nothing more you can do. It's a painful moment when you understand that the addicts' recovery must be their own decision and something beyond your control. This usually happens when they've hit rock bottom, and the pain of their self-destructive behavior becomes impossible to ignore. Relationships break and the people around them disappear, and that's often what it takes for them to finally seek help. We've been waiting for this day for almost 30 years. We're still hoping and praying that they'll find the strength to change.

Thinking about it now, I guess that's why I'm so passionate about helping other people who are struggling with addiction. I've seen firsthand how it destroys lives and families. However, I also know that there's so much strength and resilience in people, even in the face of the toughest circumstances.

I ended up in relationships and situations much earlier than a typical teenager. At the age of 13, I had a grown man living with me. I got pregnant at 16, and it was a wake-up call. I realized I needed to change my path.

My daughter, Kaleeyia, has been a blessing in my life. She's now 25, and we're incredibly close. She's been my rock through many challenges. I'm so grateful for her, but the struggles didn't end there. My boyfriend at the time, who was also the father of my child, was incarcerated when I was only 2 months pregnant. I was left alone and terrified.

Despite the challenges, my siblings and I made it through. We leaned on each other and learned to survive. We saw the worst of addiction and the toll it took on our family, but God was with us every step of the way. He gave us strength and perseverance we never knew we had. If you're facing a storm, let it be a chance to grow closer to God. Embrace the humility it brings. Let go of your old ways and open yourself up to His love. It won't be easy, but it's the path to true healing and wholeness.

Here are some things that helped me along the way, and I will share the advice with you:

1. **Recognize your wounds:** Where are you hurting? What traumas have left scars?
2. **Acknowledge them:** It's okay to feel pain. Don't suppress your emotions.
3. **Seek healing:** Give yourself permission to move on and release the past.
4. **Practice self-care:** Nurture yourself physically, emotionally, and spiritually.

If it doesn't serve you, let it go. It doesn't exist. It doesn't belong to you!

I'm still working on this myself. As I type this, I'm realizing how much physical pain I've been carrying that is likely connected to the emotional weight I've been holding onto for years. It's a journey but one worth taking. There are great resources out there to help you on your healing journey. I recommend "Chasing Roots" by Shalandor Johnson. It helped me understand how to address the root causes of my issues and not just the symptoms.

God is faithful. He'll meet you wherever you are and guide you through your storms. Be ready for transformation. It might be messy, but it's the path to a more authentic, whole life. The key is that you need an open and teachable heart. In other words, you just need to be ready. My circumstances humbled me to the point that I was ready for whatever God needed to do in my heart. I have longed desperately for transformation in my life. I refuse to settle for a mundane and lifeless existence, and so should you.

10 ....It's In Your Storm

Chapter Two
It Was All a Setup

I met James through a mutual friend back in 2014 and we both were single, but neither of us were looking for a relationship. It just happened. He was still dealing with trauma from his childhood, but it was nothing that he allowed to destroy what we were building. We fell in love, and in almost two years we were married. During our relationship, we gave each other nicknames. We called each other King and Queen, and people in the community still refer to me as Queen. When I first met James, people were warning me about him. I would hear things like, "He is crazy," or "You better be careful with him." Little did they know, God was working on him. The man they once knew had turned his life over to Jesus. "The man upstairs will always take care of us," he would always say. When I met him, he was already in a good loving church home called House of Mercy in Houston,

MS. He was already headed in the right direction. After we dated for a while, I learned a lot of his story. He shared with me that he had recently been released from the State Hospital, and he had moved from Indianapolis, Indiana. It was right after the most trying time of his life when he found Jesus, an awesome church family, and a wife and kids to call his own. James was so content and happy in life. He always kept in touch with his family back home in Indianapolis. He loved them so much. God had given him the life that he always wanted and dreamed of. His words were always, "If God never does anything else for me, He has done enough," and he meant that. He never imagined his life turning around like it did. He had built a good relationship with his older kids, and he always spoke so highly of his sons. His boys were something special to him. He also had a daughter that he cherished. He met her mom when she was only six months old, and he loved her as his own.

James and I meeting was best setup for both of us. He changed my life tremendously. He made me a stronger person, and he taught me and the kids a lot. I always felt sometimes he was so hard on us, but now I see what God was doing for me and the kids. He sent somebody to build us up because we were going to need to be tough for a time like now. Everything he taught and instilled in the kids is coming in handy during one of the darkest times of our lives. We were together for a short period of time, but we had some awesome times together. We traveled a lot to Amusement/Water Parks. We were still going on dates up to his passing. Our two favorite places to eat were Texas Roadhouse and Cracker Barrel. He always made me so comfortable whenever I was in his presence. I can remember leading up to his death that he had become so humble, and he was at peace with life. I never really gave it a thought until after the incident. I began to look back at how God had really transformed him. Here is the content broken into multiple sentences while keeping the original wording intact:

He had become so humble and patient, and I even witnessed him use the words "I'm sorry," which were not words he used to anybody but me. He was fixing broken relationships he had with people, and he was checking on people that he hadn't spoken with in a while.

The beauty of James' story is that God took the worst of sinners and made him a chief example of His grace.

If you happen to feel so broken and messed up right now, always remember that there is still hope in God's arms. You may think that you can't handle your situation and you may find yourself so lost and empty, but this struggle that you are facing is not the end of your story. God will restore your life. Hold on to His great love for you because He will perform great miracles in your life.

On April 1st, I lost my James (he went to be with the Lord), but there were 7 other lives saved on that day in that

EXACT SAME HOUSE WHEN THERE WERE NO WALLS STANDING! God spared our lives, and I will dare not acknowledge that. I've learned that sometimes GOD allows us to go into storms rather than out of them. Sometimes He disrupts our little comfortable world and allows us to face storms that we have no control over! It's been in my storm that I have learned my strengths and who I am. I could never have learned in a comfortable place in my life. So I want to tell you, IT'S OK TO GO THROUGH THE STORM. YOU'RE NOT IN IT BY YOURSELF.

James' testimony: "I am always amazed at my how life is. It's been almost 10 years since I've been in Mississippi. I was at the end of the road when God told me to come back to where I came from. I didn't want to come back to Mississippi because I loved Indianapolis. I had been there my whole life. My family was there, and I love them with all my heart. I didn't want to leave them, but God wanted something more for me. I always wanted a wife that would love me for me and respect *me for the man I knew I was: A great man, a king! Today I can say I got the love of my life. She means the world to me. Not before God, but here on Earth I always got someone to talk to. She always thinks about me and the kids before herself and she's my best friend always"*

James Dean.

Are you in a storm right now? Is your faith being blasted by wind and waves of uncertainty? Watch for Jesus to reveal Himself during your storm.

Kelsay Dean... 17

CHAPTER THREE
When The Lights Are Out

I always wondered, "If I'm serving God, shouldn't my life be easier and not harder?" Maybe I just automatically assumed that was the case (or maybe I secretly hoped that I would be the exception). I had to learn the hard way that when God uses people for His glory, He often does so through trials rather than comfort. My reality check has been that if I want to be used by God and for His glory, I must be prepared for His methods! There is no way around it! Are they hard? Absolutely! Nevertheless, I would never trade any of my trials because of what God simply did through them. ~Remember, pain is not without purpose.

I will never forget March 31, 2023. James and I woke up as we would on a normal day. We both worked at the same place but on this week, he was working night shift, and I was on days (my normal shift). James had just gotten off work that morning, and I was headed to work while the kids were getting ready for school. We kissed and said, "See you later." We talked throughout the day after he had gotten a few hours of sleep. He had a part-time job at the local Walmart in our hometown. He went to work that Friday at 1p.m. I was sending out text messages to my family and friends about the impending bad weather that had been forecast to remind them to be safe. I also called James at work that day to remind him that bad weather was on the horizon. I also took him lunch on his break. We sat in my car and talked like always. Later that night, he was so tired. He had worked his full-time job all week, and now he was working his part-time job. He made it home around 10:30 p.m. I reminded him again of the storm that was on the way. He really didn't take it seriously, or he was thinking just like me that everything would be fine like always. Surely enough, a thunderstorm arose. It was raining badly, and I could hear the wind blowing. On our local news station, the weatherman was giving updates on possible tornado sightings. We had no clue that one was scheduled and headed in our direction. Our lights went out, and we had no power. Our pastor called James and told him to get his family in a safe place and James responded, "We are in our safe place; God is going to take care of us." Around 2 a.m. (April 1, 2023), I was still up and waiting for the storm to pass and of course, he was back asleep after the call with Pastor. I heard the trees blowing, and it was raining harder against our mobile home. Suddenly, I heard the train sound that I have always heard people speak of, and I told James to get up because the storm was here. His words were, "It's here?" I responded, "Yes, baby, it's here!" His next question was, "Where are the kids?" I responded to him, "I have already put them in the tub in their bathroom." He took off running and I don't know exactly where he went, but I can almost assure you that he was running to check on the kids. I ran to our closet and got on my knees and covered my head with my hands. I repeated over and over, "HELP, JESUS, HELP, JESUS! I SHALL LIVE AND NOT DIE! I SHALL LIVE AND NOT DIE!" I closed my eyes and then BOOM! The tornado engulfed our mobile home, and it picked James and me up and threw us in the front yard. I can remember everything just crumbling apart. It all happened in a matter of seconds. That night, I could feel angels hovering over us to protect us. We were hollering out to God for help, and He helped us! Our neighbors found us all scattered outside of our mobile home that was once standing. When they found me, I was thrown several yards away from where our home once stood. James wasn't too far from me. The kids were scattered in the yard as well. One of our girls came to where we were laying, and I asked her about the rest of the kids. She informed me that they all were in our son's truck safely. I asked her about James, and she said he was beside me, but he was not saying anything. I told her to go lay on him and pray over him, but she was too afraid to do it. She laid with me and began to pray. I tried getting up to go to James, but I could not move my body. I tried scooting, but I didn't realize how bad my condition was. I couldn't move anything but my head, neck, and arms. It was still raining, and debris was everywhere. There were trees toppled over in various places. Our home was gone! It was demolished! Finally, after what seemed like an eternity, neighbors and first responders came. They found all the kids inside of my son's truck. They put James and me in an ambulance together. I could see the first responders working on him. I could hear them counting and saying, "CPR." I was praying to God to just let him make it. "Lord, just let him live," but in my mind, I was wondering if this was it. Was this what God had been trying to prepare me for? Prior to this day, God had come to me several times on several occasions while driving down the road and in our bed at night to let me know that James didn't have long to live. I would just pray and cry and pray and cry! God was informing me that He was going to need him back. I never would accept this and as a matter of fact, I kept praying against it. I would never tell anyone because I didn't want to speak it out loud. A lot of times we can speak things into the atmosphere, and it happens. I didn't want to do that. I held on to what He said, but I was not going to tell or say that out loud. I can't remember much from that night in the ambulance. I just remember them trying to revive him, and I don't know if they sedated me or not. Even now, I desperately wish I could completely recall the ambulance ride. I didn't get to tell him goodbye. I didn't get to hold his hand or even be there for his last breath. I'm positive that he knew how much I loved him because we constantly expressed our love for one another. We even let the world know that we loved each other. Our love was such a beautiful story in my eyes. I know a lot of people are wondering, "Why did he not get us out of the house?" However, you really had to know James. He was raised old school. He was raised where you trusted God even during the bad weather. He never believed in leaving his home because he would rather take cover inside the home. In hindsight, we would have done things so differently, but apparently God's will was done.

After arriving at the hospital, I later found out that my oldest son Chrishton had suffered a concussion, and my youngest son Leonard had broken his leg. My youngest daughter Shaniya had broken her femur, and my next to oldest daughter Cheridy had broken her ankle. My niece and nephew were also with us that night. My niece lost her front teeth, and my nephew had bruised ribs.

Since that night, we have been trying to figure things out. We are still trying to make sense of our lives. Our lives have been forever changed since that early morning tornado on April 1, 2023. We lost EVERYTHING, And I MEAN EVERYTHING! There was not one wall standing of our home, but at the end of the day, we have found "JOY" in the midst of our unfortunate circumstances! My kids and I were instructed by God to cast all our cares upon Him, and that's what we have done! My kids are doing great, and they are in good spirits.

~People of GOD.... I know it looks like it will never end, but there is a rest and a joy for you if you allow GOD to carry your burdens. Why worry when God is in control? At first, we had it all backwards; we were focusing on the storm instead of the Captain

24..It's In Your Storm

that helped us navigate those tough tidal waves. It's only when we began to focus on Jesus instead of the storm that we find great joy.

CHAPTER FOUR
Do It Wounded

> **Come, let us return to the Lord. He has torn us to pieces, but he will heal us; he has injured us but he will bind up our wounds. (Hosea 6:1 NIV)**

God said, "Kelsay, you have to do it wounded. Produce anyway! Pray while you're still going through! Worship while you're still going through! Finish the book while you're waiting on the promise. You must still stay busy. I still have assignments for you to do while you're still yet wounded."

After leaving North Mississippi Medical Center in Tupelo, Mississippi, I began my therapy at Shepherd Center in Atlanta, Georgia. I received intensive therapy during my three-month stay. I was competitive, and the therapy team set goals with me to push me through my recovery. I didn't realize my injuries were as severe as they were. I just thought that if I did my therapy and worked hard, I'd be back to normal in no time. My spine and ribs were broken which resulted in a spinal cord injury. While I was in the ICU at NMMC in Tupelo, the surgeon fused four of my vertebrae together and put in two rods and 13 screws in my back as well as chest tubes. I was unable to move or do simple tasks to take care of myself.

Experiencing a spinal cord injury (SCI) is undoubtedly a new and challenging situation. It has affected almost every aspect of my life, and it's hard to put things back in order and adjust to my new reality. Being at home has been a major step in this adjustment. While it's been exciting to return to the comforts of home, it's also been scary and unpredictable at times. It's like most life-changing events - it takes time to adjust to a new "normal." For example, I was used to a daily routine before my injury. I got up each morning to go to work and take care of my children, and I had regular household chores. Whatever the routine was, my day seemed normal because I had some idea of what to expect. However, people who are newly injured must adjust to a "new normal." They often say it feels like they are doing things for the first time as they learn how to do activities differently. That feeling usually fades as you work through problems and learn how to best manage daily routines.

It is normal to have days when you feel down or bad after an SCI. Sometimes depression happens soon after the injury. In a few cases, depression begins sometime later. Mine came months later. For almost a month after being home and three months into my SCI, I have been asked over and over… "Kelsay, are you walking yet?" Everyone failed to realize that mobility isn't the only issue people with spinal cord injuries experience, but it's the only thing onlookers see. Spinal cord injuries cause bladder and bowel dysfunction, loss of or changed sensation, chronic pain, neuropathic nerve pain, spasms, a weakened breathing system, pressure sores, and more. I also must manage a lot of medications. Every spinal cord injury is different. People are quick to judge, but no one knows the full story.

I was literally fighting to keep my mind because I was so used to James being at home with me. I couldn't sleep at night, and the enemy would cloud my mind with thoughts until I felt like I was losing it. Some nights I would be consumed with thinking about the night of the storm and how much I missed James. I reached out to my pastors, Pastor Stan and Lady Shae, and they gave me the scripture Philippians 4:8 and I found peace in holding on to God's Word.

I want to encourage you, "Don't be powerless against spiritual torment in the night." Satan is certainly cunning and knows just when to attack! Many of his plays are set in motion and they're not when we're alert and strong, but they come when our defenses are down. Thankfully, God never leaves anyone to be the devil's doormat. Even in your sleep, you don't have to be defenseless. Nighttime is a crucial time to trust in God's power to combat the enemy on your behalf. You can sleep soundly in victory by activating God's defenses on your behalf: His cross, His blood, His angels, and His Word.

In Christ, God took our wounds upon Himself. This means that when He allows us to be wounded, we can be sure that He does it in love and not anger because we are counted as His children. If His ultimate act of love was His Son's death on a cross, then when we suffer, we know it runs in the family. God knows what it is to suffer more than we will ever know. The God who allows us to be wounded has not only suffered for us but has become the solution to all suffering and will one day usher us in the age of tearlessness.

One Sunday in 2022, Pastor Stan preached a sermon on Genesis 32 where Jacob wrestles with God. In this encounter, Jacob asks God for a blessing and in return, God dislocates his hip. For Jacob, this is a lesson in reliance on the sovereign God who wounds. This blessing came with Jacob leaving with a limp. The God who allows us to be wounded continues to teach us that He is in control, and we are not. The God who wounds is gracious and compassionate, and He is slow to anger and rich in love (Psalm 145:8). He is the very same God who heals our wounds by his own.

> **Philippians 4:8 Finally, brothers, whatever is true, whatever is noble, whatever is right, whatever is pure, whatever is lovely, whatever is admirable, if anything is excellent or praiseworthy, think about such things.**

Asking God to change your thinking is an important matter to pray about because those who fill their minds with who the Lord is, what He has done, and the things that are true, just, pure, admirable, and beautiful are blessed with a deep sense of His peace.

Kelsay Dean

The year 2023 and even now has been a year of new things for me - healing, restoration, and a lot of valleys. Even with all the valleys this year, there has been so much beauty in life once I decided to step past my fears, let go, and learn to do something new. It has not been easy. This change has been very painful. However, I had to do it, and embracing this change was the only way I could invite growth in my life. I have found out that growth is the only way to live out my full potential!

Life is calling you to embrace something new, and that requires you to let go of old ways. Grab a hold of that new thing, and trust that life has something special in store for you. Pastor Stan really helped me the day he gave me this scripture. It gave me the tools I needed to overcome the turmoil that was brewing in my mind. I would like you to ponder on this as well.

Philippians 4:8 Finally, brothers and sisters, whatever is true, whatever is noble, whatever is right, whatever is pure, whatever is lovely, whatever is admirable—if anything is excellent or praiseworthy—think about such things. (NIV)

Reflection: This verse provides a guide for what we should focus our minds on. During challenging circumstances, it's easy to get caught up in negative thoughts and worries. Paul encourages us to intentionally direct our thoughts toward what is true, noble, right, pure, lovely, and admirable.

Questions:
1. What are some specific things in your life right now that are true, noble, right, pure, lovely, and admirable? Make a list.
2. How can you focus your thoughts more on these positive things especially when you're feeling overwhelmed or struggling with negative thoughts?
3. Are there any areas of your thought life where you need to repent and ask for forgiveness? Ask God to help you cleanse your mind and focus on what is praiseworthy.
4. How can meditating on what is excellent and praiseworthy bring you peace and contentment as Paul promises in the previous verse (Philippians 4:7)?

5. Think about a specific challenging situation you're facing. How can you reframe your thoughts about this situation in a way that aligns with this verse?

Choose one action step you can take this week to put this verse into practice. This might be setting aside a few minutes each day to meditate on positive, praiseworthy things or writing down three things you're grateful for each day to help shift your focus.

Prayer: Ask God to help you transform your mind and focus your thoughts on what is true, noble, right, pure, lovely, and admirable. Pray for peace and contentment as you bring your thoughts into alignment with His Word.

34 ....It's In Your Storm

Notes:

Chapter Five
People Are Watching How You Respond

The struggle is real. There are days the grief feels like a tidal wave threatening to pull me under. The depression whispers lies: "You're not enough. God has abandoned you." In those moments, the promises of scripture can feel hollow. Yet, I've learned to reach out for my Bible and to cling to verses etched in my heart during less desperate seasons. "I believe; help my unbelief!" This has become my cry. The Word of God helps me focus and anchor my soul tremendously!

One such anchor is Romans 8:28: "And we know that for those who love God all things work together for good, for those who are called according to his purpose." This verse doesn't promise a life without pain, but it does promise that God can redeem even the darkest tragedies for His ultimate glory. On the days I struggle to see how this could possibly be true, I choose to trust in God's character rather than my emotions.

This trial has not changed the facts of my faith, but it has transformed the depth of my trust. I've learned that true faith is not the absence of doubt, but it's the choice to stand firm in the face of doubt. I've seen that in the midst of overwhelming sorrow, God is present and whispering comfort and providing unexpected moments of joy.

As I navigate the overwhelming grief and ongoing challenges of losing my husband and facing life-altering injuries, I'm deeply aware that how I represent God in my suffering matters. I'm committed to authenticity, honestly acknowledging my pain and even moments of doubt while treating myself with the same grace I'd offer to a fellow Believer. In the darkest moments, I cling to scripture as my anchor and unchanging truths that remind me of God's promises. Surrounding myself with a supportive faith community has been vital, and allowing others to bear my burdens and provide encouragement that models the body of Christ has been a tremendous help. Daily, I make the choice to trust in God's sovereignty and goodness, even when I can't see a way through the suffering. Sharing my story not to focus on myself but highlighting how God is meeting me in the trial has been a powerful way to witness to others. I continue to pray and worship as a means of expressing sorrow and frustration to God while declaring trust in Him. Seeking professional help to navigate the emotional toll has been a sign of wisdom and self-care. When depression whispers lies, I counter them with scripture and remind myself that I am loved and seen by God. Ultimately, my hope is not in my circumstances changing but in the unchanging character of God – His goodness, love, and sovereignty. This hope anchors me, and I pray it will point others to the hope found in Christ amidst their own trials.

Storms are coming my friends. As Christians, we are not exempt from life's trials – they hit both believers and nonbelievers alike. Whether natural or spiritual, these storms have the power to devastate. Yet, in the midst of the chaos, we must respond in a way that pleases God. This may be hard to accept, but **you are an inspiration**. This very day, someone looks to you as a model for navigating adversity and a reason to face the day with hope. They see Christ in you. Do not question your worth; you are here for a divine purpose. The most important lesson I've learned this year is how to find joy amidst the storms. As long as we have life, we will have problems, but it feels so good to live and let God be God! My world may be in chaos, but I still smile while clinging to God's promises. *"I know the plans I have for you," declares the Lord, "plans to prosper you and not to harm you, plans to give you hope and a future." (Jeremiah 29:11)*

I challenge you to seek God in your circumstances. Ask yourself, "What is He trying to teach me through the trials?" How can you bring glory to God as you navigate life's ups and downs? Lean into Him, grow your faith, and remember that you inspire others to do the same.

Notes:

CHAPTER SIX
The Promise Doesn't Look So Promising!

I have prayed until I had no words left, and I have cried what I feel to be gallons of tears. I have beaten my pillow up, screamed, spent many nights up trying to fix things, and nothing has happened. I'm still here, and I'm waiting on God for my promise. I have finally learned how to thank God anyway! I chose this topic because this is how I feel most days - a lack of encouragement or hope about my situation. This storm has literally had me in a chokehold. It has felt so binding at times, but at the same time, I have found peace in God to keep pushing. God has promised me His presence and His power in the middle of my difficulties, and it has helped transform me into His image. I can declare that it's been a promise worth claiming. At this point, I have learned to just be still! God knew I needed this reminder.

If I can be transparent for a moment, I will admit that my lack of staying still was one thing that God has always tried to deal with me about. I was a busy person before all of this happened. I was constantly doing something, helping someone, and running errands. I was often tired, but I loved being busy. It kept my mind off past pains and traumas. Staying busy kept me from dealing with me. When things around me were quiet, my mind was the loudest. Remembering my childhood and remembering my experience with domestic abuse was traumatizing. I hated staying still (I will discuss this further in the next chapter). Now, I have no choice. I am literally in a wheelchair without the means of being busy. Now, I have no choice but to face myself and the ghosts of my past. God was trying to heal me all along and make me whole. He had to sit me down to do so because I was too busy to allow Him to work. I'm still trusting Him for a complete turnaround any day now. I'm still in physical therapy. I have learned a lot, and I'm gaining my independence back.

Proverbs 3:5-6 says, "Trust in the Lord with all your heart; and lean not unto your own understanding. In all your ways acknowledge Him, and He shall direct your paths." This is one of the most comforting scriptures to cling to when you are facing uncertainty or difficulty in your life. Your situation or the situation around you may be beyond your understanding, but it is not beyond God's. He knows what is going on- all the how's, when's, and why's. When you do not know what to do or what will happen next, trust that He does. Follow God's guidelines and commands knowing that as you practice obedience, He is working out the rest. God sees everything that happens to you. He knows all He has protected you from. He is your source of protection. You do not need to give in to fear. It is not easy, but you can be free to be joyful and praise Him with gratefulness for this truth even when things are difficult.

I pray that I am writing something that gives you hope. My main prayer for you, if you're not already there, is salvation. I pray that you are not pulling against the storm that you are in but that you are embracing it! Lean into the pain...I know it hurts and I know it's scary, but it's also how we become better versions of ourselves. Trust that you are strong enough and wise enough to feel the pain without losing yourself. No pain, no gain! The only way to get to peace is through the pain, and salvation. (Author Unknown)

This year my primary focus is my therapy trying to reach my maximum recovery, whatever that is. I really want to learn to walk this year. As a social butterfly, I'm just enjoying being back with family and friends in MS and exploring my creative hobbies. With everything going on, it's just hard to plan for the future. I haven't finished this chapter of my life. I'm taking one day at a time and just focusing on my little improvements every day. I'm still here and still standing on my faith, and I'm still trusting God for a miracle. I pray that my story can be a blessing to someone else who may be going through a tough time. Keep pushing, keep praying, and keep trusting. Better days are ahead.

Notes:

CHAPTER SEVEN
Don't Just Be Busy, Be Effective!

Are you fruitful or just busy? Thinking about how we steward "God's" time is something we should do in every season. I think the root of the issue is that we are simply trying to do too much, and maybe this has become a bad habit or even a stronghold. We are to make plans, but hold them lightly. When planning, use a spiritual pencil and not a pen, and be open to the Lord editing your to-do list so that your work can bring Him the most glory.

Time is so irreplaceable! Every moment is a gift! The goal is not just to be busy but be effective. I spent so many years just running around like a chicken with its head cut off. If someone would call, I would go running to their rescue. I have played God to so many people over the course of my life. Some may have really needed my help, while others I honestly enabled. I felt I had to continue doing the bare minimum in their lives. I showed up for people without giving it a second thought, while at the same time I was drowning in my own mess and didn't know how to deal with my own traumas. I buried myself in other people's problems so I wouldn't have to deal with my own. Sometimes I wish I had discovered this earlier about myself, and it would have saved me so much time and finances for things that really mattered. I'm not going to allow the "what ifs" to become a distraction, though. I'm looking toward the future and what God has for me next - being more effective and not just busy. The goal is faithfulness and fruitfulness, and that simply can't be measured by how busy I am. What I know for sure is that God does not desire for us to be running around like chickens with our heads cut off. As long as I was continually busy doing good things with excellent results, lives were changed, and the Kingdom of God was furthered, I was "good." Nevertheless, my spiritual fervor had dimmed, and it became clear to me that God was calling me to come aside and be still before Him. I recommitted myself to reviving the fire of God in my own heart.

Let's seek to be about our Father's business by working and serving in a way that blesses us, encourages others, and brings glory to our God. This will look different for each of us, and it will likely require some hard decisions and changes. However, I am confident that as we seek God and ask for His guidance, He will show us the way. Let's pray for wisdom to know what to focus on and the courage to say no to the things that distract us from our true purpose. Let's strive to be fruitful and not just busy so we can bring glory to God in all that we do.

Notes:

Chapter Eight
Silence The Voices in Your Head

When you are facing hard times or things that are uncertain in your life, it is almost impossible to see God's providence as it is happening, but we can see it when we look back in reflection on the past. In other words, in times of crisis it is very hard to necessarily sense that God is present and working to bring good out of a bad situation. However, when we look back at such times, we can often see the gentle hand of God at work.

Amid our storms, we may not be able to see immediately that God is there and is leading us to peace and comfort and so much more. However, we can rest assured that this world has been set up in such a way that all can be bent and turned towards good. When we go through storms, God feels our pain and is very present with us, and He works to bring out the best in our situation.

Going in and out of stores had been too overwhelming for me; Especially Walmart since that's where James second job was. Being in crowds or going anywhere would almost wipe me out. I used to be able to tolerate going into stores and just dealing with people. I am so thankful that I have the Lord in my life. I honestly don't know where I would be if I didn't have that relationship.

I have experienced so much spiritual and personal growth trying to make it through all of this. It's been a crazy journey, but through it all, I have learned to lean into God and trust in His goodness even when I can't see the way ahead. I have learned to find comfort in His promises and to rest in His presence. When I look back, I can see His hand at work guiding me and shaping me into the person I am today. I am grateful for the growth and the lessons learned, and I am confident that no matter what lies ahead, God is with me and leading me forward.

Chapter Nine
Never Give Up on Your Miracle

There's nothing like physical pain to drive you to your knees in prayer. For over a year, time and time again, day after day, I have cried out to God for His healing power on my body, but my complete healing has not happened though there has been improvement. As a prayer warrior, I have grown weary of going to God about the same thing day in and day out. One of the hardest challenges I have found on this walk is waiting for God to answer my prayers when I urgently need Him to intervene in a circumstance that is breaking my heart, testing my faith, and was once robbing me of peace and joy.

There have been times in the past where I have been on my knees with my Bible in hand tearfully reminding God of His promises. I prayed hard when I was in a financial crisis or had a friend facing a hard life decision, even when one of my children was in trouble. I have learned that some prayers take time to fully materialize. As Psalms 40 says, sometimes we must wait for God's timing, and it is not unusual to experience what I call "intercession fatigue" when we are faithful in praying, but nothing seems to be happening. One of the greatest challenges we face as Christians is continuing to believe for a miracle when all indications are that "It just ain't happening."

Here are things to do while waiting on your promise:

1. Take time to remember how much God loves you and those you are praying for.
2. Remember all the ways God has been faithful in the past. All it takes is a memory!
3. Pray and speak the Word.
4. Be comfortable not knowing what to pray.
5. Invite others to pray with you.
6. Find peace in surrendering to the will of God.
7. Worship God.

8. "Rejoice in the Lord, always. I will say it again: Rejoice!" (Philippians 4:4, NIV).

Here are things NOT to do while waiting on your promise:

1. Don't take matters into your own hands.
2. Don't doubt what God can do.
3. Don't put your trust in people over God.
4. Let God be God.
5. Trust that God can do what He says He can do.

The journey is just as important as what we're praying for so while we wait, we should praise God for who He is and all the good things He has, is, and will do. God is going to use my wheelchair as convincing proof of the deeper healing He has given me: a settled soul, a hopeful spirit, and a confidence in grace that sustains me through every weakness I have. The God of your faith is working within you to make things whole. The dark moments of our lives last only as long as it is necessary for God to accomplish His purpose.

God sees the storm as a means of advancement. He uses the storms of life to test us and help us get closer to Him. God uses the dark, scary, and uncertain times of life for Him to demonstrate His power and for Him to get the glory and not us. God wants to use our trials to get us a little closer to Him. He has something else for us beyond the storm. When the storms of life beat us down, we need to realize that there is life beyond the storm. God is not finished with us yet. Never give up on your miracle. A promise from God is all you need!

Chapter ten
God Has You Covered

When we cry out to God in the midst of our storms, sometimes He will calm them, but other times He will sustain us through the turmoil. Your storm has a beginning, a middle, and an end. The reality is that we are either entering a storm or emerging from one. Yet, Jesus is with us in our storms just as He is with us on our sunny days. We learn things in the midst of storms, hardships, or trials that we will not learn anywhere else. So, there's no reason to panic. He is bigger than the storm! He has a plan, and His plan is greater than our feelings! His intention is bigger than any tempest we'll ever face! I don't fully understand it all. I don't fully comprehend why we had to endure the storm, but I'm grateful for one thing: I know that God has a plan for us, and His plan for us is bigger than any storm we'll ever experience!

Always remember it's in the pain that we grow. There will be times when God seems quiet in our storms, in the problems that beset our lives, and the tests and trials that come against us. If we are willing to exercise our faith and trust Him, we might find that the storms we have magnified as so immense have now disappeared or shrunk to insignificance. Sometimes God wants us to stand up and speak to them. Our faith can move mountains and calm storms! As James 1:2-4 reminds us, "Consider it a great joy, my brothers and sisters, whenever you experience various trials, because you know that the testing of your faith produces endurance. And let endurance have its full effect, so that you may be mature and complete, lacking nothing."

CONCLUSION
Life Doesn't Stop for You to Hurt

Thank you for joining me on this journey through the storms and into the sunshine. I hope that my story has touched your heart and inspired your spirit. I pray that the lessons I've learned along the way will be a blessing to you as you navigate your own trials and triumphs.

Remember, the storms of life are not your enemy, but they are your teacher. They do not break you but build you. They do not diminish you but define you. They do not destroy you but develop you. Every challenge is an invitation to trust more deeply, to hope more fiercely, and to love more unconditionally.

So let the rain fall and the winds blow. Stand tall, dear heart, and let the storm rage on. You are stronger than you know, braver than you feel, and more loved than you can imagine. The trials will pass, the sun will shine again, and you will emerge not merely weathered, but you'll be wonderfully transformed.

Thank you for your prayers, your support, and your presence along the way. May you find comfort in the comfort I've shared, strength in the struggles I've endured, and hope in the hope that has anchored my soul. Keep standing, dear one. Keep shining. Keep trusting. The storm will pass, and the sun will rise anew.

With gratitude and blessings,

Kelsay Dean

About the Author

Kelsay Anterior Dean

Kelsay Anterior Dean is the Founder of Unsilenced Hurt, a Domestic Violence Advocate Support Group, which was founded in 2017. Born in Grenada, Mississippi and raised in Reid Mississippi, a small town in Calhoun County, Kelsay graduated from Bruce High School in 2000. As the mother of 5 beautiful children and the widow of the late James Darrell Dean, her life experiences have shaped her into the passionate advocate she is today.

In 2019, Kelsay was awarded Domestic Violence Advocate of The Year, recognizing her tireless efforts to support survivors and create change. As a writer, she believes in using her words to advocate for the things she believes in. Her writing is both idealistic and realistic, reflecting her understanding that change takes time but also emphasizing the importance of standing up for what you believe in. Guided by her principles, values, and ideologies, Kelsay strives to communicate with clarity and conviction, inspiring others to use their voices to make a positive difference.

When not writing, Kelsay can be found completing physical therapy at Ascend in Tupelo MS, attending church services at House of Mercy, spending time with her children and siblings, or simply enjoying God's beautiful nature. Prior to her spinal cord injury, Kelsay worked full-time as a Team member for Hero Logistics under a contract with Toyota Manufacturing Company in Blue Springs, Ms.

Follow Kelsay via Facebook at:

Kelsay Dean / Unsilenced Hurt

www.ingramcontent.com/pod-product-compliance
Lightning Source LLC
Chambersburg PA
CBHW071230160426

43196CB00012B/2462